BLIZZARD

Heinemann
LIBRARY

Catherine Chambers

www.heinemann.co.uk/library
Visit our website to find out more information about **Heinemann Library** books.

To order:

 Phone ++44 (0)1865 888066

 Send a fax to ++44 (0)1865 314091

 Visit the Heinemann Bookshop at www.heinemann.co.uk/library to browse our catalogue and order online.

First published in Great Britain by Heinemann Library, Halley Court, Jordan Hill, Oxford OX2 8EJ, a division of Reed Educational and Professional Publishing Ltd. Heinemann is a registered trademark of Reed Educational & Professional Publishing Ltd.

OXFORD MELBOURNE AUCKLAND JOHANNESBURG BLANTYRE
GABORONE IBADAN PORTSMOUTH NH (USA) CHICAGO

© Reed Educational and Professional Publishing Ltd 2002.
The moral right of the proprietor has been asserted.

Designed by Visual Image
Illustration by Paul Bale
Originated by Ambassador Litho Ltd.
Printed and bound in South China.

ISBN 0 431 15062 1

06 05 04 03 02
10 9 8 7 6 5 4 3 2 1

British Library Cataloguing in Publication Data

Chambers, Catherine
Blizzard. – (Wild Weather)
1. Blizzards – Juvenile literature
I. Title
551.5'55
ISBN 0431150621

Acknowledgements

The Publishers would like to thank the following for permission to reproduce photographs: Associated Press pp17, 18, Corbis pp9, 22, Digital Vision p7, Ecoscene pp28, 19, Oxford Scientific Films pp5, 6, 16, 23, 24, PA Photos pp4, 11, Papilo pp8, 25, Photodisc p14, Popperfoto pp15, 20, Rex Features p26, Robert Harding Picture Library p27, Stone p12, Stock Market pp21, 29, Topham Picturepoint p13.

Cover photograph reproduced with permission of Topham Picturepoint.

The Publishers would like to thank the Met Office for their assistance in the preparation of this book.

Every effort has been made to contact copyright holders of any material reproduced in this book. Any omissions will be rectified in subsequent printings if notice is given to the Publisher.

Any words appearing in the text in bold, **like this**, are explained in the Glossary.

Contents

What is a blizzard?

A blizzard is a very fierce **snowstorm**. It happens mostly in winter. Snow falls from the clouds and strong winds blow the snow around.

Wind picks up snow from the ground. The snow is tossed into the air. The wind blows it into deep **drifts**. These snowdrifts cover roads and block doorways.

Where do blizzards happen?

Blizzards often happen on high mountains. This is because the air is colder on high ground. Some mountains are always covered in snow.

Blizzards happen in warmer parts of the world, too. They happen in North America, northern Europe and China. In these places they happen mostly in the cold winter **season**.

What is snow?

Snow is made of tiny **crystals** of frozen water. The crystals form high up in the sky. They stick together as they fall. This makes many snowflake shapes and patterns.

Snow falls in layers. Some layers are made of
dry, powdery snow. This is good for skiing.
Other layers are made of wet, heavy snow. This
is better for making snowballs!

Why do blizzards happen?

Blizzards happen when **crystals** of frozen water form in clouds. The crystals get so heavy that they stick together and fall as snow. They whirl down from the clouds, making a **snowstorm**.

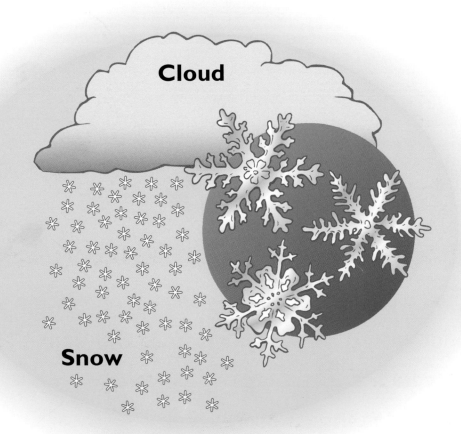

Cloud

Snow

A cold wave of air rushes in behind the snowstorm. These freezing winds blow the snow all around. When snow is blown by strong winds the storm is called a blizzard.

What are blizzards like?

Blizzard winds make the air icy cold. The thick snow makes it hard to see ahead. Then the snow settles into big **drifts**.

It is dangerous to drive through a blizzard. The
snowflakes stop the driver from seeing the road.
The road gets slippery with the icy snow.

Blizzard in the city

The city of Milwaukee lies next to a huge lake in the USA. In the winter of 2000 the city was hit by strong blizzards.

14

No one could travel. The streets were blocked
with snow. Aircraft had to stay on the ground.
Cars were covered in snow. The edge of the
lake froze.

Harmful blizzards

Blizzards can stop people from reaching hospitals and schools. Trucks that carry food cannot get to the shops.

Blizzards make thick layers of snow on the mountains. These layers can slip. Then an **avalanche** of snow tumbles down. This can bury people and animals.

Preparing for blizzards

Weather forecasts can often tell when a blizzard is coming. The weather forecasters give out weather warnings. Then people can prepare for the blizzard.

Roads can be prepared for a blizzard. Road
workers spread salt on the roads. This melts
the snow as it falls on the road. The snow
cannot settle.

How do people cope with blizzards?

A **snowplough** is used to clear roads after a blizzard. The snow is pushed to the side of the road. The snow piles up at the edge of the road.

People wear thick coats to protect them from blizzard winds. A hat is very important for keeping the head warm. Boots help people to walk through the snow.

Coping with blizzards – Inuit

This boy is an Inuit. Inuit are people who live in the cold **Arctic region**. This boy wears layers of clothing that trap warm air. He has a fur-lined hood and snow boots to protect him from the cold.

Some Inuit can build houses quickly out of blocks
of snow. This protects them from blizzards. Inuit
can catch fish by making holes in the thick ice
that covers the sea.

How does nature cope?

Lambs are often born under the snow in a blizzard. The mother's body melts the snow around it. This makes a warm space to keep the lamb alive.

This mountain flower has hairy leaves. They let in light but protect the plant from blizzard winds. Many plants die in winter. Their roots or seeds lie safe underground.

To the rescue!

In the mountains, trained dogs sniff for people buried in the snow. Rescuers follow the dogs. Then the rescuers push long poles into the snow to find the people.

People have to be very careful if they are driving through a blizzard. Sometimes there are accidents and rescue services have to pull cars out of the snow.

Adapting to blizzards

The big roofs of these houses protect people inside from the snow. The snow falls away from doors and walls.

This is a **snow lodge**. It was built in wild
mountain forests. Walkers can shelter inside
when there is a blizzard. They can find food
and make a warm fire.

29

Fact file

◆ The north-east coast of the USA gets very bad blizzards. On 6 March 2001, 30 inches (76 cm) of snow fell in just a few hours. People were warned that the blizzards were coming. So they bought all their food before the snow fell.

◆ Strong blizzard winds can blow snow on the ground into snowballs. These are called 'snow rollers'.

◆ Every **crystal** has a different pattern. There are many crystal shapes. Some are like stars. Others are like plates. Some have flat arms. Others have **hollow** arms. These crystals join to make snowflakes.

Glossary

Arctic region area around the North Pole. The area around the South Pole is called the Antarctic region.

avalanche when a thick, heavy layer of snow slips down a mountainside

crystals small shapes of frozen water

drift snow that is blown into a thick mound

hollow empty

season months of the year that have the same type of weather

snowplough vehicle that can clear the snow from roads

snow lodge hut that shelters walkers in a blizzard

snowstorm heavy snow and strong winds brought by large dark clouds

weather forecast information about the weather that we will get in the future

Index